CHAPTER GUIDE

CHAPTER 1
CASH-STRAPPED OR CASH-RICH? IT'S YOUR CHOICE

> *"Money is better than poverty,*
> *if only for financial reasons."*
> *– Woody Allen*

It's Tough Out There

How will you ever save enough money to buy a car, pay for car insurance, health care, pay off student loans, update and replace your smart phones every two weeks (or every time you lose them), rent an apartment, buy a house, raise a family and somehow enjoy life along the way? To find the answers to these common concerns, you've come to the right place.

We aren't diving into piles of money like Saturday morning cartoons would have liked us to believe as children. In fact, we are barely staying afloat. These are some sobering statistics reported February 24, 2011 by the online site *MSN Money Partner*. "In 1970, the average private wage earner made $312 per week (in 1982 dollars). In 2004, the average worker earned $277 per week (in 1982 dollars) – and it's still falling. That means once you factor out inflation, the average wage earner in 1970 brought home about 18 percent more than the average wage earner today."

The report continues that, "Even if you adjust for inflation – and even if you take into account the crash of the housing bubble from 2007 to today – the median price for a home in the U.S. has gone up more than 50 percent since 1970. Remember, that number accounts for inflation, so what that number actually means is that the cost of a home requires 50 percent more of a person's paycheck than it did in 1970. (Furthermore) the cost of an undergraduate degree today is roughly 30 percent higher than it was in 1970."

And it concludes that, "In order to compete in today's workforce, a young person often must have items that weren't needed in 1970, including a cell phone, a computer, and home Internet access. Often, in the search for work, it's very difficult for a young person to compete without these extra expenses."

The bottom line is that it's tough out there in the working world – and this means, for young people especially, the ability to manage money and start saving for their future as soon as they land a good job is more critical than ever before. We live in a "Y.O.Y.O." economy, which stands for, "You're On Your Own." And yet most parents seldom choose to discuss the important life issues of money management and saving for a rainy day with their children (perhaps because *their* parents didn't show them the way). Most schools and colleges also fail to include these subjects in their curriculum even as they prepare students today for the highly competitive job market.

But all is not lost, despite the doom and gloom flowing from so-called personal finance "experts." This book is aimed at filling that void – and providing a counterweight to all the bad news. Its purpose is to help working Americans in their 20s and 30s win back the dream that is on the verge of disappearing and create a very different financial future for themselves. It signals a *fundamental shift in how young people should think and go about managing their money and saving for their future.*

A huge part of that will have to do with taxes! You may say, "Taxes? That's my parents', my grandparents' and their accountants' concern. I don't make enough money yet." But you would be wrong! Taxes are a subject for **you** to focus on, beginning *right now*, as your parents and grandparents probably wish they had done when they were your age. You have that incredible opportunity right now, so don't waste it. Plus, you have access to new tax-free options that were not available years ago. Remember this: The more you pay in taxes, the less you keep. Taxes will be a key factor in how much of your lifetime earnings will actually be left for you and your dreams.

To modify a saying I use when talking to people across the country, I want you to pay less taxes so you can have MORE, MORE, MORE – more money for you to enjoy NOW, more money for your FUTURE, more for your loved ones, and more of it **TAX FREE!**

Write this down: Tax Free is KING!

Fund Your Future is, therefore, for today's generation of younger workers like you – those who are just entering the workforce from college, starting a family, or simply have a desire to build a solid financial future by turning what might seem like a hopeless uphill battle into a potential mountain of cash. Youth is a huge financial edge here, and this book will hopefully motivate you to take control of your financial future by cutting Uncle Sam out of the equation and developing your OWN plan, not the government's plan.

Now don't get me wrong. I'm not advocating against paying your taxes. Our country needs tax revenue in order to stay solvent. What I am advocating against is paying more in tax than needed. To paraphrase a wise old head: "I'm proud to live in a country where I can afford to pay taxes. But I could be just as proud for half the money." **How about you?**

ASK ED

Q: "Ed, I'm 28 years old and have been working about five years. Taxes are the last thing on my mind. I base my budgets, my livelihood, on my take-home pay, what I bring in, not what I "make." I don't know how to get the most out of the tax code or use taxes to my advantage at tax time, because taxes are foreign to me. As a young, single individual I don't even put much effort into my tax returns, in the form of write-offs, etc. compared to older, married individuals. For a person like me, in my economic status, why should I even be concerned about saving on taxes?"

ED: It's true that taxes play a much larger, more visible role in the lives of families, older individuals, homeowners, and parents than young people who base their entire retirement, savings and day-to-day portfolios on the figure they see on their paychecks. But...not to answer your question with another, who would you rather have spending your earnings—you or the government? Understanding the tax code is just like any other daily task you implement to save more of your hard-earned money. By working with someone who understands the complex code inside and out to advise you on your financial affairs *(see Chapter 6)*, you can arrange your finances to get more spending power for each dollar you earn, which is especially important when you are just starting out and trying to stretch your earnings! You will quickly see more wiggle room to put some of that spending power aside today in a savings or investment account so that you have the ability to make larger purchases in the future or use the funds to support yourself later in life. You wouldn't pay to see a concert without any knowledge of the band's music, would you? The same holds true with taxes. Knowledge is power. The tax code impacts you from your first day of work through your golden years.

As headlines have shown, companies can take away workers' savings plans (and retirement security blanket) in a heartbeat. Younger workers *know* they must rely on themselves to build and preserve their savings and are looking for another way. The pages that follow provide it.

The Power of Compounding

The financial services industry and certified public accountants like myself have long advised taxpayers to choose a tax-deferred savings plan (the take-the-cash-now; pay-tax-later plan) – and for good reason: for decades, tax-deferral (i.e., tax-*infested*) planning has been the *only* game in town. But the advent of the Roth IRA and its companion Roth 401(k), Roth 403(b) and Roth 457(b) plans have changed that. (For detailed explanations of these different savings plans, *see Chapter 2*.) By paying tax now on what you save rather than deferring the tax on your savings until well into the future when the tax rates are uncertain, you may lose some relatively small and short-lived tax deduction upfront but substantially *prosper* down the road.

For example, let's say your career is rolling full-steam ahead and you are already in the 30 percent tax bracket (federal and state). That means a contribution of $4,000 to a traditional tax-deferred savings plan is worth only about $1,200 in savings on your current tax bill. That's barely more than $23 a week! You probably blow more than that on Happy Hour "specials" or making in-game purchases on the latest iPhone app. Remember, this money isn't a refund, it's a *deferred tax* that you *will* pay on that $4,000 eventually – plus the tax on all the interest the $4,000 will generate over the years – when you start withdrawing money from the account.

If instead, you give up the $23 deduction for a greater reward later, the exchange is clearly much better, especially over time, through the power of compounding (the percentage of interest growth on both the principal and accrued interest). In fact, Einstein, most famous for his work with the power of gravity and the equation $E = mc^2$, once called the power of compounding interest the most powerful force in the universe.

Over the years, numerous studies have shown that people who develop good money-saving habits early in life are more financially successful as they get older. Even small contributions made at a young age can add up to big savings in the future thanks to the time they have to grow and compound.

ASK ED

Q: "I'm making $30K, I have student loans, a car payment, just starting out, how can I afford to save? All of the money I make, I need."

ED: You have to think about the process as paying yourself first – meaning before making out your bills or paying tax to the government. Maybe this requires going out to eat only one time a month or cutting out the morning Starbucks coffee, but a good starting point for paying yourself first may be to put $50 or $100 a week in a jar away from sight until it contains $500. At that point, put that money into a Roth IRA for continued **tax-free** growth. Rinse and repeat. It isn't easy and it requires sacrifice, but why not reward yourself for all of your hard work, especially since you will be writing checks each month to companies for your car payment and your student loan provider.

Your Greatest Moneymaking Asset

Time is the greatest moneymaking asset an individual can possess, and young people have more of it than anyone else. This is your time and you need to capitalize on it now, *while your age is still a powerful advantage*. Time itself is what makes the tax-free planning approach work, and the proof is this: the creation of the Roth IRA is now more than a decade old so we have many years' worth of dollars-and-cents evidence to confirm what I'm saying.

For example, let's say "Roy" started saving smartly when he was 25 by contributing the maximum allowable amount to a Roth IRA each year to a Roth IRA each year for say, 14 years. As of now, he has contributed $49,000 to his Roth, which, after compounding at an average rate of 6 percent over the fourteen years, is now worth $72,058. Had he opted for the traditional tax-deferred approach to saving (a 401(k), for example) with the same interest rate, Roy would have accumulated the same amount of money. In addition, he would have received a tax deduction each year for his contributions. On the surface, the traditional approach seems like a better deal. But let's run some simplified numbers.

Let's say the hypothetical combined tax savings over the same fourteen years from 401(k) contributions would have been identical: $700 ($9,800 worth of tax deductions over fourteen years at a hypothetical tax rate of 20 percent). It would appear that betting on the tax-free planning approach with a Roth instead (as Roy did) was a poor choice. But Roy knows himself. That $9,800 in tax-deferred savings over fourteen years from a 401(k), which averages out to $700 per year, would be great if he were disciplined enough to have invested those funds. But Roy knew that he, like most people in his age group, would probably have used that money to either buy some big-ticket item he'd had his eye on, go back-packing through Europe or to pay off last year's holiday credit card balances, thereby losing every penny of his theoretical tax savings. But now comes the *really* bad news.

If Roy had opted for the 401(k) instead of a Roth IRA, never put another dime into the 401(k), and left that $72,058 to grow for 25 years, at the same 6 percent average, then his $72,058 would have grown to $309,263. But remember, *that pile of cash is not all his*; every dollar he will withdraw is subject to income tax, and the rate of income tax he will pay is determined by whatever his tax bracket will be when he starts withdrawing (typically at age 65).

In other words, he has to share it with his Uncle Sam, who isn't even a relative! Nevertheless, Uncle Sam gets a chunk of his "nephew" Roy's sacrifice, savings and investing efforts. If Roy's tax bracket at that age is 35 percent, then $108,242 in that account will still belong to the IRS, which he will have to pay back upon withdrawal. On the other hand, if Roy never puts another dime into a Roth, the same $309,263 *is all his* — bought and paid for long ago when his Roth was worth only a fraction of that amount.

Which account would you rather have? You can see why Roy chose the **tax-free planning alternative**. Because less tax equals more for him! And that's math we can all enjoy.

ASK ED

Q: "How do I take the steps to be cash-rich for the future when I'm cash-strapped in the present with hefty grad school loans to pay back?"

ED: Start small. Stay basic. Saving does not have to be a grand experience where you save more than you can afford. Saving is also about living within your means. OK, you can't afford to put away $500 a month just like you can't afford a Mercedes, but, every little bit counts. Do what you can. Save what you can and start now. Doing nothing just prolongs the situation and creates tougher hurdles later on. Get in the groove now, at your pace. This is not a race, it's a marathon. Action even in moderation always defeats inaction in the money management and savings game. (*See Chapter 3* for more strategies and tips.)

Plan Proactively

The down-the-road results Roy has already achieved are not obvious to most people when they start out contributing to a savings plan and laying the foundation for their future. But in order to start right, you need to look down the road so that you can plan proactively.

ED SLOTT'S
ELITE
IRA
ADVISOR
GROUP™
Find an advisor at
IRAhelp.com

As with most things in life, when it comes to saving, it's a lot easier to avoid mistakes than it is to fix them after they happen. Proactive planning is one of the best ways to make sure those mistakes never happen in the first place. It's kind of like driving. If you just looked right in front of your car as you drove down the road, imagine how many potholes you'd hit and trees you'd crash into. But by looking ahead, even though you're already moving towards your destination, there's time to alter your course if necessary. The same principle applies to your planning. By focusing on what may lie ahead financially, you can avoid those potholes too. And when you do, you will see that the tax-free approach to saving wins, hands down.

ASK ED

Q: "Ed, I'm already contributing to Social Security through payroll deductions. Isn't that a savings account?"

ED: Yeah right! Dream on. Social Security is not so much a savings account as a form of *insurance* – for you. It protects you from the ramifications of no longer being able to work due to old age, disability, or death. What are these ramifications? To quote the Economic Policy Institute's publication, *A Young Person's Guide to Social Security*, "You can end up with nothing – because you made low wages and could never save, because you never had a pension or 401(k) benefits through your job, because you were laid off during a recession and had to burn through your savings to make it to the next job, because you became ill and had to stop working, because your child became ill and you had to stop working, or because another Enron went belly up or the stock market crashed and wiped out half of your actual retirement savings." The publication goes on to say that if, "you are 22 years old and starting your first job in the fall of 2011, you have 45 years before you can claim full Social Security benefits. On the day you begin your first job, someone who began work 45 years earlier, in 1966, will retire. In his (or her) 45 years, this worker witnessed seven recessions, lived through inflation, stagflation, oil shocks, oil rationing, the stock market crash of 1987, the savings and loan collapse, the bursting of the 'dotcom' bubble, the bursting of the housing bubble, the stock market crash of 2008, and the bailout of AIG, the financial industry, and the auto industry;

saw unemployment climb above 10 percent twice; and all this over a time period with slowing wage growth for the bottom 50 percent and the decline of traditional pensions." With that kind of history as a guide, the likelihood is that you will need to save, save, save also.

The big shock for tax-free planning investors, of course, is the loss of the tax break upfront, but it only comes as a shock because of the conventional "wisdom" today that tax-deferred saving is the best available option. With a traditional IRA, 401(k), or 403(b), contributions are taken out of workers' paychecks before they pay any taxes on them. That lowers today's tax bill, although Uncle Sam eventually gets his due when withdrawals are taxed as regular income. When the piper comes to collect, today's conventional "wisdom" maintains that the retiring investor will "likely" be in a lower tax bracket than when he or she was working. But given today's huge and growing deficits, soaring health care costs and other economic factors, that "likelihood" is no longer so likely; tax rates *will* increase. They must in order to keep the country from drowning in a sea of red ink. And tax-deferred savers will be paying the freight! Tax-deferred savings are easy pickings for the government. They are the low-hanging fruit just waiting to be taxed at the highest tax rates. That won't change. Distributions from your IRAs and 401(k)s receive no special capital gains rates or other tax breaks. They are taxed at what the tax law calls "ordinary income" tax rates – the highest tax rates in the land! Tax-deferred simply means "pay later." Tax free means "pay now" by giving up the tax deduction.

So, yes, you give up the tax deduction, but that small payout grants you tax *freedom forever.* Furthermore, as Roy was well aware, the tax savings from the deduction are, in most cases, spent rather than invested. But even if you did invest the tax savings, the tax-free method of funding your future will still yield better results because, with some exceptions *(see Chapter 2), you will never have to pay tax on any withdrawals!*

ASK ED

Q: "Are there situations where a tax-deferred savings plan might be preferable to a tax-free plan?"

ED: Generally a tax-deferred plan is preferable if you need the deduction on your tax return. If your salary is $50,000 and you are putting $5,000 into your 401(k), your W-2 from your employer will show $45,000 as taxable income so you will find yourself paying less income tax and that extra money can (and should) be socked away for retirement. If you make an IRA contribution, you can deduct the full amount (dollar-for-dollar) from your taxable income.

The Roth 457(b) has become an option for state and local governments that offer traditional 457(b) plans. The Roth 401(k), the Roth 403(b) and the Roth 457(b) do not have the same income contribution limitations as the Roth IRA (where contributions are prohibited once adjusted gross income reaches $206,000 for married couples and $139,000 for singles in 2020).

As a result, many American workers now have access to a Roth account and tax-free planning in some form.

ASK ED

Q: "I am working but my spouse will be a stay-at-home mom until our newborn starts school. Can I make a Roth contribution for my spouse?"

ED: Yes, as long as your earned income is more than the amount of your Roth contribution, you can make contributions for both yourself and your spouse. (For more on the ins and outs of the Roth IRA, and other qualified savings plans, *see Chapters 2-5.)*

No More Uncertainty

Starting today, you can build a potentially staggering tax-free savings plan by capitalizing on (1) your age (the younger you start, the surer the result) and (2) tax-free Roth planning. In our system today, you either create your own plan, or you're given one by the government. (Hint: Yours is usually better!) Ultimately, all plans come down to three simple steps; figure out where you are now, figure out where you want to be, and then figure out the best way to get from here to there. *Fund Your Future* will show you how to:

1. Determine whether contributing to a Roth is right for you.

2. Explore innovative ways to raise the cash to pay upfront taxes.

3. Make the most of Roth compounding over time.

4. Determine if/when to convert from a traditional tax-deferred savings plan to a Roth IRA, Roth 401(k), Roth 403(b) or Roth 457(b).

5. Tap your Roth IRA early, without penalty, for necessity or emergency cash – to cover college tuition expenses, buy a home, pay certain bills, and even avoid foreclosure.

6. Take advantage of the latest tax law changes governing Roth IRAs and Roth 401(k), Roth 403(b) and Roth 457(b) plans to save even more.

7. Protect your future "millions" from creditors, divorce, bankruptcy, lawsuits or other problems when you are ready to collect.

With this saving strategy, you can start out with very little and potentially become a millionaire someday just by keeping up your Roth contributions, converting to a Roth when the time is right (see Chapter 4), and making use of Old Man Time to collect a tax-free fortune at the back end.

ASK ED

Q: "Ed, I'm already contributing to a 401(k) at work. Can I also take advantage of the tax-free planning concept by contributing to a Roth IRA?"

ED: Yes. Your participation in a plan at work – 401(k), 403(b), 457(b), etc. – does NOT impact your ability to contribute to a Roth vehicle, as well. (For more on Roth and other qualified plan eligibility rules, *see Chapter 2.)*

Fund Your Future takes the uncertainty out of future tax rates

because with tax-free planning…when you start withdrawing from your Roth IRA, every dollar is tax free (assuming you are at least age 59½ and the account is at least five years old); thus, you are *assured a zero tax percent rate when you collect!*

Do all the projections you want, but you cannot beat a **zero** percent tax rate. You are going to love keeping more of the money you make. It starts now.

CHAPTER 2

THE NAME OF THE GAME IS *INCOME*

> *"You can only be young once. But you can always be immature."* – Dave Barry

It's no secret that American workers rank pretty low on the savings barometer. It's also no secret that *younger* American workers rank even lower on that scale than many of their elders.

In fact, according to a survey conducted by the online investment service TD Ameritrade, more than 50 percent of twenty-to-thirty-something Americans have no qualified savings plan set up either at work or on their own. Furthermore, of young workers who do have employer-sponsored savings plans available at their workplace, fewer than a third of them elect to participate in those plans (see Figure 1) – and, adds the tax information service CCH, just 4 percent of those who do participate max out their contributions *even if their employer offers a corresponding match.*

Company 401(k) participation				
	Participate	% of pay	Avg. balance	Median balance
Ages 18-25	31.3%	5.6%	$3,200	$1,280
Ages 26-41	63.1%	7.2%	$31,240	$14,730

Figure 1

The likely reason stems from your age and priorities. You are just starting out in the work world so you're not even thinking now about saving for your future. Why should you (tongue in cheek)? Retirement is as far off in the distance, you may say, as the events of World War II are far off in the past. In a sense this is true – which is why I use the word "saving" rather than the words "retirement planning" throughout this book.

To younger ears, "saving" has the ring of immediacy – even urgency – to it that "retirement planning" simply does not. But time does fly and the future does seem to have a habit of arriving sooner than we anticipate. And if you see yourself in any of those statistics I've just cited, you've got some financial CPR to do – that is if you hope to afford to kick back and enjoy your future (where the name of the game is income) whenever it comes rather than continuing to put in those sixty-hour workweeks just to stay afloat.

Even a few dollars put aside each week or month can grow into a substantial nest egg over the long term. It all depends on your readiness to start saving now through a qualified savings vehicle inside or outside the workplace – because every dollar you save today will only become more valuable to you down the road as it's given more time to grow, and grow, and grow.

ASK ED

Q: "Ed, are CDs or interest-bearing accounts a valuable source of saving?"

ED: They are valuable as an immediate source of cash. Most financial professionals advise you to have 3-to-6 months of salary stashed in an interest-bearing savings account. The funds are available in a medical emergency or if you lose your job. In that respect, they are not long-term 'saving' tools, but a necessary component of your overall financial well-being. These accounts should not be used as a primary source for retirement planning...**oops, I mean saving**.

More About Tax-Deferred Versus Tax-Free Savings

Tax-Deferred

A qualified, "tax-deferred" savings account is just that. The dollars you put away plus the interest earned are taxed at a later date when you start taking withdrawals (usually in retirement). In many ways, the tax-deferred approach mirrors going to the dentist with a toothache. You put the trip off in hopes the ache will just go away. But it just gets worse, and when you finally do go to the dentist, you hear, "Hmm, looks like the infection's spread; we'll have to take out this tooth and these other four too!"

Tax-Deferred (Until Withdrawal) Accounts	
Traditional IRA	for anyone who qualifies
401(k)	for company employees who qualify
403(b)	for governmental, educational, and other organizational employees who qualify
457(b)	for state or local government or tax-exempt (under IRC 501(c)) organization employees who qualify

Figure 2

You can put money in a traditional IRA (Individual Retirement Arrangement) and deduct your contributions, regardless of your income, if you are single and are not covered by a workplace retirement plan such as a 401(k), 403(b), or 457(b) pension plan. The same is true if you are married and neither you nor your spouse participates in any workplace retirement plan.

If you are covered by a 401(k) or other workplace retirement program, your IRA deduction begins to phase out at adjusted gross income above $65,000 (for singles) or $104,000 (for married couples). It ends completely at $75,000 (singles) or $124,000 (married). These limits are for 2020 and are indexed annually for inflation.

The rules dictating whether or not you are covered by a workplace retirement plan can be tricky. The best way to know your status is to ask your employer directly or see if the "Retirement plan" box in Box 13 of your W-2 is checked off for the year in question. Employers are required to provide this information annually on the W-2 form.

If you are not covered by a company sponsored plan but your spouse is, your contributions phase out between $196,000 and $206,000 (for 2020) of adjusted gross income. But fear not, you and/or your spouse can always make a non-deductible contribution to a traditional IRA without any phase-outs provided either of you has a sufficient amount of "earned income" and you report such a contribution to the IRS. This term is generally defined as wages of any sort that you receive as payment for work, but it also includes self-employment income.

Take a look at the tables in IRS Publication 590-A for the rules on Traditional IRA deduction eligibility and for the limits for the current year. You can access this publication at this web address: https://www.irs.gov/pub/irs-pdf/p590a.pdf or just search for "IRS Publication 590-A." If some or all of the contribution is not deductible, you should file Form 8606 with your tax return to accurately account for the after-tax contribution to the traditional IRA. Most tax return preparation programs do these calculations and print the right forms, assuming of course that you provide the right input. You might be better served asking a tax advisor or CPA about this. They usually handle this while preparing your taxes.

Tax-Free

Here you shell out income tax upfront on the dollars you put away in a qualified Roth 401(k), Roth 403(b), or Roth 457(b) savings account at work or a Roth IRA outside of work – but that upfront tax can be a small price to pay for the potential tax-free windfall on those dollars *plus all the interest they have earned* when you start taking withdrawals.

As with tax-deferred savings, you or your spouse must have earned income in order to contribute to a Roth IRA, but other eligibility rules for these accounts differ somewhat from their tax-deferred competition. For example, the ability to contribute to a Roth IRA phases out at adjusted gross income between $124,000 and $139,000 for singles and between $196,000 and $206,000 for married couples. These limits are for 2020 and are indexed annually for inflation. Remember too that your participation status in a workplace retirement plan has no bearing on your ability to contribute to a Roth IRA.

As their names imply, the Roth 401(k), Roth 403(b), and Roth 457(b) combine features of the traditional 401(k), 403(b), 457(b) and the Roth IRA. As with the traditional company sponsored versions of these savings plans, you can set aside up to $19,500 in a Roth 401(k), Roth 403(b) or Roth 457(b) account each year, plus (as of this writing) another $6,500 way, way down the road when you turn 50. $19,500 is the maximum amount you can defer to all employer plans combined in one year, and that is the limit for 2020.

Tax-Free (On Withdrawal) Accounts	
Roth IRA	for anyone who qualifies
Roth 401(k)	for company employees who qualify
Roth 403(b)	for governmental, educational, and other organizational employees who qualify
Roth 457(b)	for state or local government or tax-exempt (under IRC 501(c)) organization employees who qualify

Figure 3

Roth IRAs Versus Roth Company Plans

There are some key differences between Roth IRAs and the Roth accounts you may have through your 401(k), 403(b), or 457(b) plan. Read on to learn about three of the biggest ones.

Difference #1 – Access to Your Funds

Regardless of the type of plan account (i.e. regular 401(k), Roth 401(k)) you may have, when money is held within an employer plan, access to the funds is often limited. Sometimes, the limitation is due to the Tax Code and IRS Regulations that apply universally to all plans, but quite often, a plan's own rules can place further limitations on when you can access your own funds.

Roth IRAs, on the other hand, have no such legal restrictions. While a Roth IRA investment may place some restrictions on you (i.e. a penalty for withdrawing your money before a certain date), the Roth IRA rules allow for Roth IRA money to be accessed at any time. Regardless of how old you are or how long you have held the account, **Roth IRA contributions may be withdrawn at any time, for any reason, tax and penalty free**. So there is absolutely no risk to making Roth IRA contributions. Hopefully you'll keep your hands off your Roth IRA money so it can grow tax free, but if you need it, you can at least tap your Roth IRA contributions any time you want – no taxes, no penalties, no questions asked.

This is often a big benefit, particularly if you are young and need access to your money for significant purchases, such as a down payment on a home *(see Chapter 5)*.

DID YOU KNOW?

You can open a Roth IRA at almost any financial institution and invest it in almost anything – stocks, bonds, certificates of deposit (CDs) or mutual funds. Whereas in a traditional 401(k) plan, you are limited to the options selected by your employer. Of course, fewer options can be more appealing to some folks – but what if those options turn out to be high cost and under perform?

Difference #2 – Required Minimum Distributions (RMDs)

Age 72 is a long, long, long way off, but I still thought you should know this: Although it may be a Roth account, a Roth 401(k) – or another designated Roth account (defined as a Roth account maintained by a company plan) – is subject to company plan rules. As such, at age 72 you must begin taking distributions from your Roth 401(k) accounts, just as you would from traditional 401(k) accounts. If you are over 72, still working and own less than 5 percent of the company you're working for, then you may be able to delay RMDs from the plan of the company you are working for until the year you retire.

If you plan to use your Roth 401(k) money to supplement your retirement income, the RMDs may not seem like that big of a deal, but if your goal is to leave the account alone to maximize its value down the road, the RMDs will significantly hinder that effort. But RMDs are no big deal and certainly not a reason to avoid contributing to a Roth 401(k) at work. RMDs at age 72 can easily be avoided altogether simply by rolling your Roth 401(k) funds to a Roth IRA before the year you have to begin taking RMDs.

Roth IRAs have no RMDs during the Roth IRA owner's lifetime. So if you have a Roth IRA and don't need the money, you can leave the account alone to grow tax free for as long as you'd like. The extra growth can help provide more tax-free money later in life or can be used to provide a tax-free legacy for future generations. Keep in mind, however, that beneficiaries of Roth IRAs are subject to RMDs, but those distributions are generally tax free. You probably can't even imagine now that, yes, you will have beneficiaries one day. That means that people who may not even exist yet are relying on you!

Difference #3 – Eligibility to Make Contributions

One big advantage of designated Roth accounts over Roth IRAs is that there are no income limit restrictions that would prevent you from making contributions. In contrast, if your 2020 income is over $206,000 and you file a joint return ($139,000 for a single filer), you are completely phased-out of making a Roth IRA contribution.

On the other hand, Roth IRAs have a major edge over designated Roth accounts as well – far more people have access to them. As long as your income is below the applicable threshold for your filing status and you have earned income, you can make a Roth IRA contribution. Things like your age and whether or not you are covered by a company plan have no effect. On the other hand, few people have access to designated Roth accounts at work. In fact, recent surveys indicate that only about 20 percent of 401(k) plans have a Roth component.

ASK ED

Q: "Ed, what can I do if my employer doesn't offer a Roth?"

ED: Then the heck with him (or her)! As long as you qualify, you should start your own Roth IRA. 'I' after all stands for 'Individual.' You may be better off in the long run. Remember, unlike a Roth 401(k), Roth 403(b), or Roth 457(b) plan, a Roth IRA is not subject to plan rules and you will have immediate access to your contributions at any time, although I don't recommend that unless an emergency arises. Another option: Start your own company and create your own Roth 401(k)!

Inertia seems to be the new way of thinking about workplace retirement plans. Employers and investment firms recognize that most people just don't spend a lot of time or effort on their 401(k) accounts, even after a number of wild years in the financial markets. Many studies paint a similar picture: most 401(k) participants just don't tinker much with their accounts.

It can be tough to get people, especially young adults and those earning modest pay, to sign up for 401(k) plans, contribute money and manage their investments. However, once they do sign up they tend to put their accounts on autopilot. They generally don't change their investment elections or increase their contributions, even when their compensation rises. From an investment perspective, this could be a good or bad thing. Only time will tell.

Recognizing that individuals in general do have inertia when it comes to participating and managing their investments, companies that put together 401(k) plans are stressing features that require minimal effort. These may include "automatic" provisions related to enrollment, contribution increases, and suitable default investments if participants don't make their own selections. Of course, participants always have the option to "opt-out" of these automatic provisions, but studies have shown that most do not, which is not surprising because it would take effort on their part to do so.

Employers and investment firms are learning to give 401(k) participants what they need, and not much more. It seems that the most effective plans are simple, understandable and capable of running on inertia.

Roth IRAs Versus Traditional 401(k)s

When it comes to saving, people tend to be more concerned about investing – in stocks, bonds or various mutual funds – than if the savings plan they choose, whether it's a 401(k) or other employer sponsored plan or a Roth IRA, best serves their future financial goals.

I always tell young savers that apart from their respective tax-deferred versus tax-free characteristics, the big distinction between a 401(k) and a Roth IRA is this: The match. If your employer matches your 401(k) plan contributions, you would be crazy not to take advantage of a 401(k). An employer match amounts to free money, so you should put in as much as you need to get the full match. But if you don't get an employer match, or if you have already received the full match and want to save more, a Roth IRA is often the better option.

If you opened a Roth IRA and a 401(k) and invested in them identically and in a disciplined manner, guess which one will provide you with the most income down the road? OK, don't guess. Let's look at an example instead provided by the global investment management firm T. Rowe Price.

Let's say you invest $1,000 each in a Roth IRA and a 401(k) plan (with no company match), earn an average of 8 percent a year, and hold on for 30 years. Your tax rate remains fixed at 25 percent. In year 30, you withdraw all of the money. At that time, you will be left with $10,063 from the Roth IRA, all of it tax free. After paying tax on the 401(k), you have only $7,547. Clearly, the Roth beats the 401(k) by 25 percent.

Now let's say you are a very unusual young saver and you take the $250 you saved in deferred taxes when you started your 401(k) and rather than blow it on a new iPhone, you invest it in a separate account at 6.8 percent (which is 8 percent adjusted for the 15 percent capital gains rate). After 30 years, you would have an extra $1,799. Add that to your 401(k) balance, and you'd have $9,346. The Roth is still better by almost 8 percent! The problem with this example is that the tax rate stays the same.

Of course, there is no real way to accurately predict what your income tax rate may be in the next five years let alone in another

20 or 30 years. If you could, I'd hire you in a second! So, my general rule of thumb is to take your tax break when your tax rate is at its highest, not lowest. Today's income tax rates are the lowest they've been since the 1950s. If your hunch is that by the time you retire tax rates will be even lower than they are now, you might choose the 401(k) plan because it gives you a tax deduction today.

You may also believe that even if tax rates do go up over the next thirty-plus years of working full time, you'll still be in a lower bracket when you retire because you'll obviously be earning less. But remember, all the money you take out of your 401(k) plan is counted as *income*. And should you start up a small business, decide to work part time or receive a large inheritance and invest it, you could generate additional taxable income and wind up having a tax rate the same or even higher than before.

Here's another rule of thumb: The longer you have to save, the better the Roth IRA becomes; the growth that builds up over many years in a Roth will be all yours, whereas the growth in a 401(k) plan will be shared with the government. So, if you believe tax rates will go up (as I do) and think your tax rate will be higher 30 years from now than it is today, you might want to choose the Roth IRA since it gives you a bigger tax break tomorrow instead of a smaller one today.

ASK ED

Q: "So, would I be better off with a new Roth 401(k) or staying with a traditional 401(k)?"

ED: It all comes down to what your tax rate is now and what it may be in the future coupled with the number of working years you have to contribute and invest. Younger workers in their twenties and thirties are best suited for Roth 401(k)s because they literally have decades to build up their savings, which can then be withdrawn in retirement tax free. That's a plus given today's tax deficits and the likelihood that their taxes will go up in the future. But even if I'm wrong and you're in a lower tax bracket when that time comes, you'll still be glad you're able to withdraw from your Roth 401(k) tax free.

My Building Blocks to a Tax-Free Future

Tax-deferred plus Social Security was your parents' and grandparents' retirement savings plan, but it should not be yours. By following my building blocks to savings success ("Contribute," "Convert," "Collect") in the next three chapters, you will not only better protect your accrued assets but grow those assets into a potential tax-free fortune by applying some recommended methods of disciplined saving and letting time itself do the rest.

- **Building Block #1: Contribute.** Shows you how to start taking advantage of the exponential growth and tax-free savings opportunities of a Roth IRA by opening one right now – or, how to open a Roth 401(k), 403(b) or 457(b) if available where you work. It will explain how to make and how to fund regular contributions, and even offer tips on how to come up with the cash to do so – in other words, how to spend now to gain more later by setting up a tax-free plan and contributing the maximum allowable each year.

- **Building Block #2: Convert.** Perhaps you have a 401(k) where your employer has agreed to match your contributions up to a certain amount, but now that amount has been reached, or your company has experienced a downturn and can no longer match contributions; the advantage of "free money" is gone, and you would be better off converting to a Roth IRA or Roth 401(k) if your plan allows. This building block shows you how to transfer current tax-deferred funds into a tax-free account if you are eligible as soon as a conversion makes sense. I also offer tips on how to lower your tax cost of converting to make converting a better move, and how to determine if you have creditor protection for your Roth account(s).

- **Building Block #3: Collect.** This last block focuses on taking your money out of your Roth for varying purposes. It would seem that this process should be simple enough: just take your money, tax free. But to avoid incurring taxes or penalties, withdrawals must meet certain requirements in order to be considered "Qualified Distributions" by Uncle Sam. Using real-world examples, this chapter will go into all requirements for being a Qualified Distribution (for instance, the funds must have been held in the account for more than five years), and pitfalls to look out for so that you (and your spouse and children down the road) will enjoy the fruits of your Roth wealth-building as profitably and headache free as possible.

If you use these building blocks, you will create what I consider the *perfect retirement savings account* by setting up your down-the-road nest egg so that tax on distributions is substantially reduced or outright eliminated forever.

DID YOU KNOW?

When you begin drawing Social Security, you may have to pay tax on some of your benefits if your income is high enough. Money you take out of a 401(k) increases your income and, therefore, can increase the tax you pay on Social Security benefits. But money you take out of a Roth IRA is not counted toward income in this calculation and therefore will not increase the tax you pay on Social Security benefits.

CHAPTER 3

BUILDING BLOCK # 1: "CONTRIBUTE"

> *"A goal without a plan is just a wish."*
> *–Antoine de Saint-Exupery*

A Brief Refresher

Okay, to refresh your memory, here in a nutshell are the rules once more for contributing to Roth IRAs and company plan counterparts. These limits are for 2020 and most are adjusted annually for inflation. You can contribute up to $6,000 annually per person to a Roth IRA if your yearly income is below $124,000 (for single taxpayers) or $196,000 (for married couples filing jointly). The $6,000 annual contribution limit can be apportioned any way you want between your Roth and traditional IRAs. At a minimum you should make a token Roth IRA contribution to start the running of the five-year holding period. For example, a 2020 Roth IRA contribution made as late as April 15, 2021, starts the five-year holding period as of January 1, 2020. In most cases, married persons who file separate returns cannot make Roth IRA contributions.

Roth contributions are permitted without regard to participation in a 401(k) or other company sponsored tax-deferred retirement plan, or to age – thus, you don't even have to wait until you're age 20 to start saving; children with summer jobs can fund a Roth IRA based on their earnings, too.

Now, with that out of the way, here's the tough part about funding your future, and I can already hear the refrain: "But, Ed, I'm too strapped to contribute much of anything! Where do I find the money?" Well, read on. I'll show how to start taking advantage of the exponential growth and tax-free savings opportunities available by opening up a Roth IRA right now – or, if available where you work: a Roth 401(k), Roth 403(b) or Roth 457(b).

ASK ED

Q: "Ed, I keep hearing about the importance of building a rainy day emergency fund. Can I do that in a Roth?"

ED: You can use your Roth IRA contributions as an emergency source of cash for a down payment on a house or to pay for graduate school, BUT I advise you to keep your Roth IRA for later in life if you can find the money somewhere else, like in a bank savings account. If you do decide to take money out of your Roth for an emergency or other necessity, your **contributions** will come out tax-free BUT you will pay tax and a 10 percent early distribution penalty on any interest withdrawn. For example, if you contributed $15,000 to a Roth IRA that now holds $16,500 after interest has been earned, the first $15,000 taken out is tax-free but you would pay income tax on the other $1,500 as well as a 10 percent penalty.

Paying Yourself First

Overcoming the mindset of tax-upfront is a big issue for all age groups considering a Roth, but particularly young people who are mostly concerned about holding onto as much of each paycheck as possible through deductions and other means. (Let me tell you now, this concern doesn't disappear with age.) But money can't spread its wings and grow unless you're paying yourself first. That's what contributing to a Roth (or any other qualified savings account) is really all about.

For example, let's say you want to attend that big music festival – whether it's Coachella or SXSW. Why shouldn't you attend? Of course you need to be able to relax and have fun after working all week. But do you really need to "glamp in luxury"? By deferring on the VIP passes, and instead opting for general admission and sticking the difference you save in a Roth, you can have your cake and eat it too – festival tickets and the exponential growth of a Roth – by paying yourself first. Okay, so you have to lose a deduction and pay tax on the contribution – none of this comes without sacrifice (saving isn't *free*). But paying tax on pennies that can grow into dollars – potentially BIG dollars – makes that sacrifice worth it.

ASK ED

Q: "Ed, how long can I continue contributing to a Roth IRA before I have to start taking withdrawals?"

ED: There are no required distributions from a Roth IRA during your lifetime – only after you're dead. See why it's a good deal? But once the Roth IRA is inherited by a non-spouse beneficiary (if you inherit a Roth IRA from a deceased family member, for example) there are required distributions for the beneficiary – that means you – starting the year after death. Always keep your inherited IRAs separate from the IRAs you make contributions to on a regular basis.

If you are going to spend, do so wisely – and to make memories rather than just continuing to purchase tangible things. Be smart with your money (a.k.a. purchasing fewer expensive pleasures in favor of more frequent, less expensive ones).

Do you need to have that $1,500 gym-quality treadmill with all sorts of bells and whistles to energize you in the morning? Most people wind up using it to hang things on anyway. Go for a walk or a run outside instead – the outdoors is free! That's what I mean when referring to "expensive" pleasures, but keep in mind that the buzz word "expensive" means different things to different people so plan based on your financial blueprint.

For some, paying yourself first can be as simple as putting $200 from each paycheck into a low-interest CD or money market account, while for others it can be doubling that amount and sticking it into a Roth IRA. Many young people today have two jobs, so maybe tips or income from your second job can be put away to pay *yourself* first. In many shapes or forms, paying yourself first makes you feel financially stable and keeps you financially solvent into your golden years. Funding properly and effectively in your 20s and 30s is the key to a safe and secure future. The money you set aside every two weeks to a Roth or related company sponsored plan will grow, and potentially flourish for you and your loved ones. Let's look at a couple of hypothetical examples of how well paying yourself first can pay off.

Let's say "Jake" opened a Roth IRA during high school with money he earned from odd jobs. He contributed $1,000 a year for all four years. If Jake never contributes another dollar to his Roth IRA, he will have over $85,000 in his account at age 69 assuming a 6 percent annual rate of return.

But let's assume that after he graduates from college and lands his first job, Jake goes crazy and contributes $1,000 a year to his Roth IRA for another four years. By age 69, Jake will have over $133,000 in his account. Not bad for only contributing $8,000 and letting the money do the rest of the work. Compounding never takes a day off!

OK, now let's look at a different scenario. Let's say that after Jake starts working he contributes $20 a week to his Roth IRA. That comes out to $1,040 a year. That is not a huge amount so he was able to set it aside each week. Without ever increasing the amount of his contributions and contributing until age 69, Jake would have well over $200,000 in his Roth account, assuming the same 6 percent annual rate of return.

But since Jake has the discipline to set aside $20 each week to put into his Roth IRA, let's assume as his earnings increase, the amount he saves each year increases until he is putting away the maximum – which today is $6,000 per year. Even if Jake cannot put that much away until he is 35 years old, but continues his disciplined saving until retirement, he will easily have built up over $500,000, all tax free. And that assumes he does not contribute to any other plan at work over all those years and spends the rest of the money he earned. It also assumes only a 6 percent compounding rate. Can you even imagine how much he would have if he also contributed to a tax-free Roth 401(k) at work, or received a higher rate of return? Wow! Remember that you can contribute much more to those plans. This kind of saving could easily double Jake's tax-free retirement projection to $1 million, or more – all Tax Free! That's why I love tax free, and you will too. That's why I love the Roth IRA. You never have to worry about taxes, ever. You keep what you save.

ASK ED

Q: "Ed, if I'm getting a tax refund each year, does that mean I'm having too much in taxes withheld from my paycheck every week? If so, how can I stop this and put that money to work for me by funding my Roth and other qualified savings accounts?"

ED: Yes, you are having too much withheld. Most people prefer receiving a check from the federal government after tax time because they lack self-discipline. If you do have self-discipline, you are better served withholding less. You can file a new withholding form with your employer if you choose to do so, and using that "extra" money to fund a tax-free savings account such as a Roth IRA. Remember, the IRS is paying you no interest on the withheld funds.

Now let's look at another disciplined saver named "Hope," age 25, who opens a designated Roth 401(k) plan at work. The tax code allows an employee participating in a 401(k) plan to defer up to $19,500 of their salary to the 401(k) or to the Roth 401(k) account each year. That is the maximum, and it can be split between the two accounts in any amounts she wishes. The plan is not required to allow her to defer the maximum; it can set a lower limit.

I am going to assume that Hope elects to defer $6,000 a year to her Roth 401(k) account. These funds will show up on her W-2 as taxable income even though Hope does not actually receive the money. Hope continues her contributions for six years until she takes some time off to have a family. If Hope never contributes another dollar to her Roth 401(k), at age 69 she will have over $430,000 **TAX FREE** in her account assuming a reasonable 6 percent annual rate of return.

Now let's assume that Hope returns to work at age 40 and resumes her deferrals of $6,000 a year until age 69. Hope will now have $933,285 in her Roth 401(k) account. That is almost $1 million! But it is even better than that. Like most employers, hers will match at least some of the funds she defers to her employer sponsored plan. If Hope has a dollar-for-dollar match, this puts another $933,285 in her 401(k) account (the employer match cannot go into the Roth 401(k) account). This is like free money – what could be better? Together (Hope's contributions plus her employer's match), she will have accumulated almost $2 million (and half of that tax-free) for her retirement, based on a lifetime of making small, but consistent contributions. The earlier you begin, the more it will grow.

Remember: You should never leave this free money on the table. Make sure you defer at least enough of your salary to your employer plan to get the maximum amount of the employer match. Even if Hope's employer only matched 50 cents to the dollar, she would still have an additional $466,643 in her 401(k) account. That's still a lot of free money!

Not bad, huh?

DID YOU KNOW?

Many grandparents and other relatives can set up "529 Plans" (named for section 529 of the federal tax code) to help young people with college expenses. Family members can contribute up to $15,000 a year to these plans ($30,000 for a couple) without incurring gift tax. The money can then grow in the account tax free. Family members who want to quickly get money out of their estate for tax reasons can "front load" contributions by giving $75,000 right away (or $150,000 for a couple). Front-loading in this manner will preclude the donor(s) from making any other contributions to the account, or annual gifts to the person for whose benefit the account was established, for five years. The money in the account can be used to pay college tuition, room and board, or certain other education-related expenses. As important as actually making contributions is to building a secure financial future, being aware of the contribution rules and deadlines in order to avoid potential tax headaches and missed opportunities is a must.

Keys to Disciplined Saving

Let's say your budget is so tight that you can't squeeze out $50 bucks a paycheck let alone $200. (I have my doubts, but I'll go along for now.) Where else can you find the money to contribute? How about that refund check on your income taxes you look forward to getting back each year? Instead of blowing all or most of it on some fleeting extravagance or on paying bills you should budget to pay throughout the year anyway, why not do what many Americans do? Shore up your future financial security with a financial boost by contributing those income tax refunds to a Roth or other qualified savings plan. It's a helpful first step – and you can even arrange to have this done automatically so that the money never touches your hot little hand, tempting you to spend it – i.e., it stays out of sight, out of mind.

In tax year 2006, the federal government began to allow individuals to directly deposit their income tax refunds into qualified accounts such as the Roth IRA. Previously, tax refunds could only be directly deposited to passbook savings and checking accounts.

The direct deposit of an income tax refund into an eligible account has many advantages over the old-fashioned method of receiving a refund by mail, including safety and speed of delivery. If you are

married and file your taxes jointly, you can direct that your refund go to a Roth IRA or other account owned by either you or your spouse. In fact, your refund can be split and directly deposited into as many as three different accounts. However, you are responsible for ensuring the money ends up in the right account. The IRS assumes no responsibility for taxpayer or preparer error.

Using the direct deposit option to fund your Roth IRA is not without issues. First, the financial institution administering it must accept direct deposits. Second, you must make sure to have already established a Roth IRA and that it is ready to accept your refund deposit. Third, you will need to tell your IRA custodian or trustee the year for which the contribution is to be credited. You have until April 15, 2020 to fund an IRA for 2019 and, of course, you can fund your 2020 IRA at any time in 2020, up to April 15, 2021.

Having your federal tax refund directly deposited into an eligible account is always challenging because you can never be 100 percent certain as to when the refund, and hence your contribution, will actually be made. If it is after April 15, then it can't be considered a contribution for the prior year.

Another problem can occur if the IRS makes a correction or disallows a deduction. In these cases, you may not know if you've fully funded your annual contribution or perhaps even over-funded it. If it turns out you've over-funded it, you will be subject to a 6 percent excise tax on the excess amount unless you withdraw it, along with any earnings, by your tax-filing deadline, including extensions. So, make sure to closely monitor your tax refund if it is going into your qualified Roth account.

ASK ED

Q: "Ed, when is the proper time to fill out beneficiary form paperwork? I have a Roth IRA but I am only 24. None of my friends have filled out beneficiary forms. Is it fruitless to fill out paperwork my friends call `old-people' paperwork?"

ED: Everybody should have a beneficiary form filled out regardless of his or her age. If something were to happen to you, with a completed beneficiary form, the funds in your Roth would go where you want them. Without a form, the company holding your Roth IRA or the laws in your state will determine who gets your money. Is that what you want to happen? If not, you should absolutely fill out the beneficiary form now. And you should name both a primary and a contingent beneficiary. Hopefully you will not need to use it for a very long time. But you never know. And for that reason alone you should review it annually as life events change.

CHAPTER 4

BUILDING BLOCK # 2: "CONVERT"

> *"Time is our most precious asset.*
> *We should invest it wisely."*
> *– Michael Levy*

The Right Choice

After years of income limits, Roth IRA conversions are now open to all taxpayers, including those high-income folks who stand to gain the most from such maneuvers. A Roth IRA conversion is effective the day funds are removed from your traditional IRA or other tax-deferred account and converted to the Roth. That day determines the year of conversion, even if those funds are not actually deposited in the Roth until the following year.

After the conversion, there will be no required minimum distributions (RMDs), as there are with tax-deferred plans such as traditional IRAs, and the account will grow income tax free for both the Roth IRA owner – that's you – and for your future beneficiaries.

ASK ED

Q: "Can federal employees who contribute to a TSP (Thrift Savings Program) have part or all of their TSP contributions converted to a Roth IRA, and if so, what is the best way to do it in terms of the taxes that would be owed?"

ED: Yes, TSP's are generally eligible for a Roth IRA conversion. You need to check the provisions in the plan document to determine if you are eligible to take a distribution. Factors to consider to determine when you should do a conversion would include; what you think your income will be in the year of the conversion and what you think the applicable income tax rates will be; higher, lower or the same. You also need to consider where the funds will come from to pay the tax and when they will be available. You do not want to take funds from the Roth IRA to pay the conversion tax if you can avoid it.

Basically, a Roth IRA conversion is treated as a rollover because you're shifting funds from one type of account to another. Rollovers are accomplished in one of two ways – a direct trustee-to-trustee transfer or a withdrawal and deposit within 60 days. Generally the direct transfer is the preferred method of the two. For a Roth IRA conversion, however, there is a third and better method. It's called "re-designating," and it's easier than switching banks. For example, if you have your traditional IRA with Fund Company Z, just call and say, "Make my traditional IRA a Roth IRA," and it's done! Your account is re-titled a Roth IRA (after you complete the necessary paperwork) and the money never has to be moved. The conversion is achieved instantly, and safely.

Of course, when you convert from a traditional IRA or a company plan, you will owe income tax on pre-tax money you convert, just as you do with regular contributions to a Roth. This begs the question: "Where will I get the money to pay the tax?"

One choice is to pay the tax from the traditional IRA or company plan. That's generally not a good idea, however, since then not all of the funds are working for you in the Roth IRA. In addition, if you are under age 59½, which very likely you are since this book is aimed at people in their twenties and thirties, you would be subject to the 10 percent early withdrawal penalty on the funds not converted (the funds used to pay the tax). That, of course, is a poor use of money.

If you do not have enough non-IRA funds to pay the tax on a Roth conversion, the conversion generally won't be worth it. In such cases, it might be wise to avoid a Roth conversion altogether. In other cases, though, converting smaller amounts incrementally may be the right move. Smaller annual conversions can still add up to big sums of tax-free money over time. Consistency is the key here.

ASK ED

Q: "I just started working at this position six months ago and have a 401(k) with my employer. Is it best to roll my minimal 401(k) funds into a Roth or should I wait until I have a more sizable amount of money before moving it into a tax-free shelter?"

ED: Generally you will not be able to move your 401(k) plan assets while you are still working at that specific company without penalty. The 401(k) plan document will indicate under what conditions you can or cannot move that money. If however, your 401(k) plan has a Roth 401(k) option you may be able to direct your contributions into it now, or even convert your 401(k) funds within the plan to the Roth 401(k) (an in-plan conversion).

Finding the Money

The most tax-efficient option to fund a Roth conversion is to find non-IRA cash to pay the tax. However, finding funds to pay the tax on a conversion may not be easy. When you discuss this with your financial advisor (yes, you need one; *see Chapter 6),* you might start by compiling a list of your financial assets, dividing them into four categories:

- **Cash.** This category includes already-taxed funds such as money market funds and bank accounts (but not IRA or other tax-deferred accounts). Withdrawals from these funds will not generate any tax, so all of the funds can be put to work to pay the Roth conversion tax.

- **Capital gain assets.** These include stocks, bonds, mutual funds and real estate. You may have paper profits on some of these assets, paper losses on others.

- **Tax-deferred assets.** IRAs, 401(k)s, 403(b)s and 457(b)s go into this category. If you take money from these accounts, you will owe income tax at ordinary income tax rates and perhaps a penalty, depending on your age.

- **Tax-free assets.** Roth IRAs belong in this category because they can generate tax-free distributions (after the five-year and age 59½ requirements are met). The same is true for life insurance proceeds, another potential tax-free source of Roth conversion money if you inherit from parents or grandparents who had life insurance.

Generally, you will do best to take money from one of the first two categories (cash and capital gain assets) to pay the tax on your Roth IRA conversions. Doing so will maximize the amount you can move into the fourth (and most desirable) category – a potentially **tax-free** Roth IRA.

ASK ED

Q: "To convert to a Roth IRA, do I have to put all my eggs into one savings account basket?"

ED: No. You can have as many IRA accounts as you want, including Roth IRA accounts, and you can choose from a greater variety of investments within them, leading to a diversified portfolio. Even if you convert all company plan money (if applicable) to a Roth IRA, you still get to choose from that variety of investments and diversify your portfolio within that Roth IRA.

Tap Cash

Financial advisors often suggest that you hold anywhere from three to six months worth of cash for emergencies. If you have to pay an unexpected medical or legal bill, for instance, you will appreciate having liquid assets you can tap.

What's more, as long as you're not holding your cash in a tax-deferred savings vehicle, you can draw down cash at any time without owing tax. (You might owe a penalty for a premature withdrawal from a bank CD, though.)

Therefore, your own cash reserves might be a good source of funds to pay the tax on a Roth IRA conversion. That's especially true if you are holding more cash than you really need for emergencies.

To see if you've got the cash available to tap for a Roth conversion, it's good to start by separating your balance sheet assets into three categories based on when this cash might be needed: now, later or never. Your conversion planning should focus on using the cash that will likely *never* be needed.

That cash needs to be leveraged into either Roth IRAs or life insurance, both of which have the ability to turn *taxable* money into *tax-free* money. In an environment of rising taxes, you need to be moving your cash into tax-free territory for the long term anyway, and life insurance and Roth IRAs accomplish that.

Sell Capital Assets

Other than cash, the best place to look for money to pay the Roth IRA conversion tax is within your taxable investment accounts where you may have some unrealized losses. Selling those assets can provide a bank of net capital losses. Then you can sell some of your appreciated capital assets, which can be sheltered from tax by the net losses and increase the amount of cash available to pay the taxes on a Roth conversion.

Roth conversion income is considered ordinary income, not capital gain income. Capital losses (losses on investments) can only offset Roth conversion income up to $3,000 per year or $1,500 if you are married filing separately.

For example, you cannot use a $100,000 capital loss to offset a $100,000 Roth conversion. It can only offset $3,000, and the rest of the loss is carried over to future years. Capital losses, though, do offset capital gains.

Let's say you may already have taken most or all of your capital losses. You also might have a bank of losses carried over from prior years. If so, you can take capital gains, tax free, until you have used up all your realized losses. The sales proceeds from taking profits can be used to pay the Roth IRA conversion taxes. This is what I call using the confusion of rules inherent in the tax code to work for you.

But what if you have unrealized gains but no capital losses, realized or unrealized? You might consider selling while the 15 percent maximum tax rate on long-term gains still applies. This rate could increase in future years.

In addition, using capital assets for Roth IRA conversion taxes means that the amounts left in taxable accounts will be reduced. That may mean less taxable investment income in the future and less exposure to potentially higher taxes on future investment income.

Use Life Insurance

Here's another creative strategy for finding the money to convert to a Roth IRA – use life insurance. The downside, of course, is that you will have to die prematurely for it to work. However, that is not always the case. Ask your insurance professional about permanent life insurance, which will allow you to actually grow your money tax free inside the policy and still have access to it during your lifetime if you need it. If you don't need it, it will provide tax-free income and financial security for your loved ones should you die prematurely. Life insurance of any kind is essential to protecting a young family.

I talk about funding your future throughout this book, but the use of life insurance is more about funding your family's future in case you die prematurely. Now is the time to create financial security for your *family* because you are young, presumably healthy and a life insurance policy will cost less without an extensive medical history or cost-rising pre-existing conditions. Even small premiums at a young age can produce a significant tax-free death benefit for your family when it is needed most.

Roth IRA Creditor Protection

One more factor to consider in deciding whether to convert is the issue of asset (creditor) protection. As mentioned in *Chapter 3*, many states have extended protection from creditor claims to IRAs. In some cases, however, they may not have included the same protection for Roth IRAs.

For example, in some states, protection currently applies only to IRAs created under Code Section 408. But Roth IRAs are created under Code Section *408A*. Special legislation is needed by these states to extend protection to Roth IRAs – and, in fact, most state legislatures have moved in that direction.

ASK ED
Tax Law Update

Q: If after I convert my plan or IRA funds to a Roth IRA, and the Roth funds have lost value, can I undo the conversion so I'm not stuck paying tax on value that no longer exists?

ED: No! The Tax Cuts and Jobs Act enacted on December 22, 2017, repealed the ability to reverse (undo) a Roth conversion after 2017, so all Roth conversions are permanent now. This maneuver was technically called a "Roth Recharacterization" but that is no longer permitted for Roth conversions.

That being said, as a younger person, you have a much longer time horizon to wait for a market rebound and then all the gains in your Roth IRA will be tax free forever. This still makes the Roth conversion an excellent tax move for younger workers and investors.

In addition, if market values do decline, that would be an ideal time to convert and take advantage of paying tax on lower values or to convert more funds without increasing your tax bill.

As usual, time works in your favor with a Roth conversion, so take advantage of it!

> *"Broke is normal. Why be normal?"*
> *– Dave Ramsey*

A Matter of Priority

A 26-year-old marketing associate whom I will call "Ben" had aggressively set himself up for a future windfall by contributing to a Roth IRA ever since his first summer job after his freshman year in college. He continued to fund his Roth IRA even with an entry-level salary and by now had $25,000 in contributions put away. But after several years of "sacrifice," which Ben defined as living in a studio apartment too far removed from the city's nightlife, he decided he wanted a change and set his sights on purchasing a condo within the city limits.

The problem he faced was available money. The purchase price of a relatively nice condo in a desirable area of the city started at $250,000, but Ben had been able to set aside just $15,000 for a down payment, less than the 10 percent minimum many mortgage companies desire for advantageous loan interest rates. With just one more year of saving for the down payment, Ben knew he could scrape together the remaining $10,000 he needed in order to reach $25,000 in liquid savings for the full 10 percent. But he was in the grip of "instant gratification fever," which was running high; he *wanted* to be a homeowner in the city *now*, and he felt he *deserved* it after so many years of "sacrifice."

And so he began looking at the $25,000 of contributions he had sitting in his Roth IRA, and felt it was just begging him to be of help purchasing the condo. Right then, he decided to withdraw $10,000 from his Roth IRA, which he could do tax and penalty free since the distribution would come from his contributions to the account, to fund the balance of the down payment for the condo he wanted.

Seems reasonable, right? But look at the big picture. If Ben exercised the same kind of discipline he'd shown in the past and waited that one more year, he would have been able to save enough to purchase the condo *without* dipping into his tax-free Roth IRA. Face it, Ben didn't really *need* the condo at all, let alone at that precise moment. He just allowed short-term thinking to get in the way of long-range planning when it didn't fit into his best financial picture. Now he would have to work doubly hard to make up for this major cut into the proactive savings plan he had previously stuck to so rigorously and with such discipline since college. But, of course, he now had the condo – even though the expensive nightlife he'd sought closer proximity to was now beyond his means.

I can wax poetic with warnings about "living within your means," but as this example shows, day-to-day spending is not all you need to monitor. In fact it isn't even the most important component. Normally, big-ticket luxuries and the finer "necessities" are what tempt people – young people especially – the most to consider pulling money from their Roth IRA or other qualified savings plan. Short-term vacations are luxuries that should never be funded with plan contributions because the goal of proper proactive planning is to enjoy a daily vacation long term. Cars and houses are necessities in many cases, but the *type* of car or house you elect to purchase is always a matter of choice and life priority. Right, Ben?

Tapping Roth Money Early

Roth IRA money is the best money on earth because it's tax free. It's even sacred money. That's why the worst tax move you can make is to withdraw early from a tax-free account. That's exactly the money you want to leave alone – so that it will keep growing and you will never have to share it with the IRS. In addition, the distribution rules are complicated if you tap Roth money early. But the same is true of traditional IRAs – except it's much more expensive to get at your traditional IRA money because you have to pay the income tax on the deferred amount on top of a 10 percent penalty (for withdrawals before age 59½). However, with a Roth IRA, what you've put in has already been taxed so that expense is already covered if you withdraw early. And you can even avoid paying a 10 percent penalty if the funds you withdraw are your original contributions or certain conversions and not earnings (interest accrued in the account).

Of course, to gain the most from a Roth, you want to avoid tapping into it at least until you're 59½ (or even longer), but there's nothing to stop you from withdrawing funds if you need them. Your withdrawals are treated in accordance with the five-year rules and in a specific sequence. This sequence, called "ordering rules," determines which funds come out first.

ASK ED

Q: "Is it wise to take distributions for financial hardship at such a young age when I'm ahead of the game in retirement savings?"

ED: Wise or possible? Under certain circumstances, it is possible. However, if you could afford to pay a loan over time with your current income, your Roth IRA will have the ability to continue to grow. "Ahead of the game" in retirement savings is certainly a relative term. Keep putting as much as you can in retirement accounts as long and as often as you can.

Ordering Rules

If you tap your account(s) early, the first funds out are treated as your original Roth contributions (all Roth IRA accounts are treated as one account for this rule). Roth contributions can be withdrawn tax and penalty free at any time for any reason. After all of your Roth IRA contributions are withdrawn (or if there are no Roth contributions), the next funds out are considered your Roth conversion funds, which are distributed on a first-in-first-out (FIFO) basis, meaning conversions from the earliest years are treated as the initial converted funds withdrawn. These withdrawals will be subject to the under-59½ 10 percent early withdrawal penalty if the conversion has not met the five-year holding period rules (but no tax because you paid it when you converted). Each conversion has its own five-year holding period. (This rule was put into effect to close a perceived loophole that would have allowed individuals to conspire to convert from their traditional plans and then withdraw from the Roth IRA with no penalty.) If any after-tax funds were converted to the Roth IRA, then the taxable portion of the converted funds are deemed to be distributed first, and then the non-taxable portion.

Earnings are treated as the last funds distributed from your Roth IRAs. Beware, however, that another five-year holding period rule applies to the earnings. Earnings will be subject to both tax and 10 percent penalty (unless you qualify for first-time homebuyer, disability, or another exception). In other words, you will have lost the tax-free benefits of the Roth. But after a five-year holding period **AND** after age 59½, you can take out the earnings in your Roth IRA (as well as your contributions and all conversions) at any time for any reason, tax and penalty free. This five-year holding period only runs once starting with the first Roth IRA you establish.

So, the first money out is treated as a distribution of your contributions, followed by conversions, then earnings – **in that order.**

ASK ED

Q: "Ed, I'm 28 years old and I am inheriting a Roth; how do I avoid falling into an income tax trap?"

ED: As you've already learned, Roth distributions have ordering rules. The first money out comes from annual contribution amounts. When that is exhausted, then distributions come from converted amounts. Distributions of contributions and converted amounts are income tax free since the tax was paid when the money went into the Roth account, and, they are always penalty free for beneficiaries since death is an exception to the early distribution penalty. The last money distributed from the account comes from earnings. Earnings could be taxable to you but only if the decedent has not had a Roth IRA for at least five years. Once the five-year period has ended, you are home free and all distributions will always be income tax free – at least under the tax code as it exists today.

Using Plan Money to Cover Expenses

Here's a familiar refrain I hear from young people quite often these days. "I work full-time but am also going to have a big student loan bill when I finish my masters program. I have read that I can pay for my schooling with distributions from my Roth IRA." You may have wondered this yourself.

Many individuals searching for money to help pay off college debt can find a ready source of available funds in their company sponsored retirement savings plans, traditional IRAs and Roth IRAs. Beware of the early distribution penalty trap here. Distributions from IRAs or Roth IRAs to pay higher education expenses are not subject to the 10 percent penalty when the withdrawal is made in the year of the expense. Distributions from company plans, however, are subject to the penalty. Distributions from any retirement plan, including IRAs, to pay off student loans will be subject to the 10 percent penalty, making this an expensive way to pay off those loans. Just to be clear here about the distinction;

the penalty exception applies only to distributions from IRAs used to pay for the actual education itself (tuition, etc.), **NOT** to pay off student loans.

Besides withdrawing money from these plans to pay tuition, many individuals also need funds to live on, pay bills and even avoid foreclosure. I am seeing a large increase in early withdrawals from these accounts, especially for young people starting out, as well as for the reasons mentioned above.

If you find yourself in need of additional cash, you should weigh several alternatives before raiding your retirement savings. Here are three options you might want to consider if you can't find other sources of money.

Option One:

If you participate in a 401(k) plan, consider taking a loan if it's available to you. Most 401(k) plans, and several other types of employer sponsored plans such as profit sharing plans, 403(b) plans and certain 457(b) plans, allow individuals to borrow up to one-half of their vested balance, not to exceed $50,000. Terms may vary, but most require borrowers to repay their loans within five years. The 401(k) loan typically requires no credit check and minimal paper work. You may even get a better interest rate than at a bank. There are many cautions and traps here, but one stands out: Not paying back your loan. This can trigger costly taxes and penalties at a time when you can absolutely not afford it. So, be careful here!

Option Two:

Take regular distributions from an IRA. Individuals are permitted to make regular withdrawals of equal amounts from their IRA over a predetermined period of time without paying a 10 percent early withdrawal penalty for being under age 59½, provided they adhere to an IRS sanctioned or approved schedule. **They will, however, have to pay tax on those distributions.** Generally, individuals must take their payments – known as 72(t) distributions – at least once a year for a minimum of five years or until age 59½, whichever takes longer. You get a regular stream of income for an extended period of time, but you must be careful as the IRS imposes tough penalties on individuals who don't abide by their pre-arranged withdrawal schedules. I want to lay all options on the table, but this is **NOT** a great one for someone in their twenties or thirties since you will have to maintain the payment schedule for 20 or 30 years and the distribution amount will be small since you have a long life expectancy. This is one time in funding your future where your young age works against you.

Option Three:

Tap a Roth IRA. Student loans can be a big burden after graduation. It might make sense to take some or all of your Roth contributions to offset education expenses. You can take out your contributions without owing any tax or penalty on the distribution. A withdrawal of converted amounts might be subject to the early withdrawal penalty if they are withdrawn before the five-year holding period is met or before you are age 59½, whichever comes first. A separate five-year holding period applies to each conversion you make. If you take out any earnings on your account, you will owe income tax on the earnings. You can avoid the 10 percent early distribution penalty on the conversion or the earnings as long as your distribution is less than the amount of your higher education expenses (not your loan payment) for the year you take the distribution.

As already noted elsewhere in this chapter, however, you must be 59½ before you can withdraw the earnings in the account, tax and penalty free. The five-year period for this rule commences on January 1 of the tax year for which you fund your first Roth IRA either by an annual contribution or conversion. You might want to think twice before using this option. While withdrawals from a Roth IRA are generally tax free, you could be giving up many years of tax-free growth.

ED SLOTT'S
ELITE
IRA
ADVISOR
GROUP™
Find an advisor at
IRAhelp.com

ASK ED

Q: "Ed, are there tax-free ways to free up and build funds for buying a newer car, to save for trips, or to advance my education by paying for more schooling with a Roth or other means?"

ED: What you contribute to a Roth IRA, you can take out without tax, but you are negatively impacting your future by doing so. You have to weigh whether it is more important to have that new car today or to fund your future. You can make an argument for education as you are expecting a return on your investment down the road, but using tax-free funds to take a month-long trip to Europe isn't too on the ball, financially speaking.

"Savings" nest eggs exist to help insure a comfortable financial future for their owners. Taking early withdrawals may put that in jeopardy, so I always recommend that you should investigate other options available to you before using these savings for your future early. Unfortunately, for some individuals there are no other options. If you find yourself in this predicament, make sure you seek assistance from a qualified financial advisor who can help you devise a tax-efficient withdrawal strategy and help you avoid the pitfalls inherent in any of the strategies presented here (see *Chapter 6*).

ASK ED

Q: "Ed, how and when could I use some of my Roth savings to put a down payment on a house?"

ED: The answer is tied into the Roth ordering rules. If you contribute $5,000 for five years, you can take out $25,000 for a down payment with no tax or penalty. You can take out converted amounts without tax or penalty five years after the conversion. If you take out the converted amounts within the five years, you will generally have to pay a 10 percent penalty on the amount you take out. If you take out earnings (the interest gained on the money), you will owe tax and penalty on the amount you take out. The exception (to the penalty only – you will still pay tax on any interest withdrawn early) being if you are a first-time homebuyer, and this is capped at a lifetime amount of $10,000.

CHAPTER 6

TWO (OR MORE) HEADS ARE BETTER THAN ONE

> *"I took advice from none but the best. I listened, how I listened! That's how I finally became my own expert."*
> *–Peggy Guggenheim*

Not for Do-It-Yourselfers

"Paul," a 25-year-old web analyst, was in-between jobs when he made an after-tax contribution (he took no deduction for the contribution) of $5,000 to his IRA in 2015 and another after-tax contribution of $5,000 in 2016. There was just one problem with Paul's contributions – he had no earned income for those two years. You must have earned income in order to make an IRA contribution (even a Roth contribution).

Paul discovered this problem in 2017 so he did the logical, easy thing. He took a distribution of $10,000 out of his IRA in early October. Problem solved, right? WRONG! If Paul had worked with an educated financial advisor, instead of attempting to correct this mistake on his own, he would have saved himself a lot of time, anxiety, and money.

Paul's distribution did correct his problem for the 2015 contribution of $5,000 but not for his $5,000 contribution in 2016. Why not? The rule states that you have until October 15th of the year after the excess contribution to remove – with net earnings (or losses) – the amount of the excess contribution. Paul did not tell his IRA custodian that he was removing an excess contribution, and he did not take out a net amount. Therefore, he only took a normal distribution for $5,000, which did not fix the problem. Because of his second error, he owed another year of the 6 percent penalty tax and still had an excess contribution.

Let me re-emphasize a point I made at the very beginning of this book. We live today in a "Y.O.Y.O." economy — You're On Your Own, remember? Rarely have people felt so helpless in the face of financial forces few seem to understand. They seek wisdom – good, solid advice and counsel and sound expertise from people who are genuinely dedicated to helping them improve their investment strategies and plan wisely for the future.

Financial planning is not a do-it-yourself business – not anymore (assuming it ever was). And yet where do you turn to find the professional guidance and support you need when just about everyone out there who calls himself or herself a "financial advisor" claims to be an expert on all money matters? To paraphrase a quote by noted financier Warren Buffet, it's when the tide goes out that you discover who's really wearing a bathing suit and who isn't. What we're discovering today is that many so-called wizards of financial planning – the gurus, the bankers, and the brokers who call themselves "experts" – are skinny-dipping. They're all about pushing the products and services their companies want them to push and not about what's best for you. But in fairness, I know that some advisors are investing in education in this complex area because they want to do the best job they can for their clients. That's the kind of advisor you should be working with – an advisor that values continuing education.

Still, if you are serious about proactive saving and funding your future, you need a seasoned professional financial advisor, one who is not only up to speed on the top-rated stocks, bonds and other investments, but equally knowledgeable about all arcane tax laws, rules, regulations, contribution and withdrawal issues that can sink the best-laid plans faster than you can say "Mickey Mouse."

Funding your future is about more than just saving enough money for the years when you'll be working less. There are a wide range of complicated issues that need to be considered, including taxes, withdrawals, insurance, and other planning strategies. You need financial help. Here's what a financial advisor who's an expert in traditional as well as Roth IRAs and other qualified savings plans can do for you.

If you find the right financial advisor, you'll be less likely to worry day after day about whether you've done enough with your investments. Once you and your advisor create a financial plan, your advisor also will help you stick to it. And if the advisor has carefully thought through what you need to do and you've implemented the plan, you're less likely to monitor the Dow Jones Industrial Average or S&P 500 each day. Those are short-term concerns. Instead, you'll be thinking long-term.

Your Roth IRA is now (or will be soon) your most valuable asset. A qualified financial advisor is trained to manage portfolios as they grow in size and ensure that different asset categories in your portfolio are allocated properly to achieve your stated goals. Qualified plans such as IRAs and 401(k)s have highly complex tax rules that, when maximized, can save you or your estate from paying much more than necessary in taxes.

Nobody wants to miss out on tax law changes that can benefit him or her. Only an educated financial advisor stays up on such revisions. It is the job of your financial advisor, in tandem with an estate attorney and accountant, to provide financial security for you **and your family**, minimizing tax issues, maximizing protection and assisting in the transition of assets from one generation to the next if the need arises.

So, where do you look?

Finding the Right Advisor

The first step in achieving this success is to educate yourself, which you are doing with this book.

The second is to come up with a list of questions to ask a financial advisor during any initial consultation. A great place to start is the 10 Questions listed in the back of *Ed Slott's Retirement Decisions Guide: 2020 Edition* (IRAHelp, 2020). You will want to make sure any financial advisor you're considering is educated in the complex rules governing financial planning – and that he or she continues to invest in that education because these rules are always changing. Here's a sample question I would ask: "When was the last time you went to a seminar on IRA or retirement distribution planning?" The advisor might respond, "Oh, I go all the time." This should immediately arouse your bull s*** detectors. So, very innocently you say, "Oh, that's interesting. Could you show me the course manual from the program?" If you see a "deer caught in the headlights" look on the advisor's face, you immediately know you've got a problem.

Another good question to ask is, "Do you have any books on this topic?" And the advisor might say "Oh yeah, I have a book. I have Ed Slott's *"The Retirement Savings Time Bomb and How to Defuse It."* Then my bull s*** detector would prompt me to ask to see that book. If the spine of the book cracks when you open it, you know that's the first time that book's been opened – and I would run! These are among the questions you can ask to get a sixth sense of whether the advisor is really at the top of his or her game or just a salesman – a stock-jockey.

Remember, a financial advisor works for YOU, so an initial appointment should serve as a job interview for that financial advisor. A list of advisors that train with us can be found at www.irahelp.com. You can search for an Ed Slott-trained advisor closest to you by just entering your address and searching with our Google Maps feature. These advisors are members of Ed Slott's Elite IRA Advisor Group[SM].

Another of the most important qualifications of a financial advisor is the ability to explain those complex matters to you in terms you can understand. No matter whom you hire, eventually that person will be recommending investments and possibly tax strategies for you. If that person is unable to explain what the investment (or strategy) is and the rationale for you owning or following it, or if you cannot understand the explanation, or the advisor seems to grow impatient with your questions, there may be a communication problem, and that's a big red flag.

Anyone can call himself or herself a "financial advisor." But the one you want will at least be subject to professional standards – as indicated by one or more of these specific designations next to their names: CFP® (Certified Financial Planner®), CFA (Chartered Financial Analyst), ChFC® (Chartered Financial Consultant®) or CPA (Certified Public Accountant).

Of course, certification does not guarantee competence, but professional designations such as these do indicate at least a standard of professionalism, education, and accountability that you will need.

ASK ED

Q: "How do I know if a financial advisor is being honest about his or her certifications?"

ED: Just because a financial advisor claims to be certified by a professional organization doesn't mean it's true. In the wake of all the recent financial scandals, it's now clear that you have to do a little due diligence of your own on the background of anyone you consider hiring to handle your money. How do you do this? (1) Verify that the advisor has actually earned his or her credentials by calling the organizations that award certification. Also confirm with the organization that the advisor continues to satisfy ongoing educational requirements, that complaints have not been filed, and that the advisor has not been disciplined. (2) Consider hiring an online background-check firm or agency to verify your advisor's education degrees, any legal cases pending, liens and even dangerous levels of personal debt.

Involve Yourself in Your Finances

Some people turn their financial affairs over to advisors without ever giving them a second look. This is a very poor strategy. Never lose sight of the fact that it's your future you are funding and, therefore, your future that is at risk. No one can possibly care about that more than you.

Never use the "ignorance of youth" credo as a crutch; instead leverage your age to your advantage. Time is the single biggest asset on your side. Use it wisely, educate yourself now and surround yourself with a financial team that will efficiently move your money from FOREVER taxed to NEVER taxed.

As I illustrated earlier, the name of the game is income, yet no matter what number is on your paycheck, with the proper savings plan you can have more than enough to begin proactively funding your future. Once you have a savings blueprint, you can start building your financial future by contributing to an employer sponsored retirement account to take advantage of a company match (if applicable) and a tax-free savings vehicle such as a Roth IRA. Again, remember the axiom that tax free is KING! And as Mel Brooks has said, "It's good to be king!"

Especially in these times of historically low tax rates, it is wise to move as much money as possible from tax-deferred (tax-infested) accounts to tax-free territory, paying the tax now on conversions and sitting back as the money grows tax free for life!

Finally, while these tax-free accounts best serve your financial future by letting them grow, and grow, and grow some more, you can "collect" your money if the need arises by following a very specific set of rules outlined in this book.

Nevertheless, as I have shown, it's also important to know your limitations and to seek help from an advisor who has specialized knowledge and training. Roth IRAs and other qualified accounts are unlike any other type of assets. Without proper education, even the most seasoned financial advisor, CPA, or attorney can make a seemingly small mistake that could wind up costing you your fortune.

ASK ED

Q: "Ed, I'm just starting out saving (with a Roth IRA), do I need an insurance agent or an estate attorney?"

ED: You need an insurance agent if you are interested in purchasing life insurance to take care of your family, and an estate attorney if you are drawing up a will or a trust. Once you begin saving, you are building an asset that you will want to protect and plan for.

So, now you have the information you need to start building your OWN plan, not the government plan, and taking ownership of your financial well-being. Your dreams as children, your aspirations as teenagers, your goals as recent college grads are possible with some sacrifice, patience, and a proactive approach to *Funding Your Future*.

ABOUT ED SLOTT

Ed Slott was named *"The Best"* source for IRA advice by the Wall Street Journal.

He is a nationally recognized professional speaker and has starred in several nationally aired public television specials including the most recent, *"Retire Safe & Secure! with Ed Slott (2020).*

Slott created *The IRA Leadership Program™* and *Ed Slott's Elite IRA Advisor Group*SM, which were developed specifically to help financial professionals earn recognition as leaders in the IRA marketplace.

Mr. Slott is an accomplished author of many financial and retirement-focused books, including most recently *Ed Slott's Retirement Decisions Guide: 2020 Edition* (IRAHelp, 2020) and *Fund Your Future: A Tax-Smart Savings Plan in Your 20s and 30s* (IRAHelp, 2020). Slott also publishes *Ed Slott's IRA Advisor*, a monthly IRA newsletter. He is a personal finance columnist for numerous financial publications.

As a thought leader in the retirement industry, Slott is often quoted in *The New York Times, The Wall Street Journal, Forbes, Money, Kiplinger's, USA Today, Investment News* and a host of additional national magazines and financial publications. He has appeared on numerous national television and radio programs. Mr. Slott is also a consultant to financial information websites.

He is a past Chairman of the New York State Society of CPAs Estate Planning Committee and editor of the IRA planning section of the *CPA Journal*. Mr. Slott is the recipient of the prestigious *"Excellence in Estate Planning"* and *"Outstanding Service"* awards presented by The Foundation for Accounting Education. He is a former Board member of The Estate Planning Council of New York City and an Accredited Estate Planner (AEP) distinguished.

For more information:

Website: www.irahelp.com

Email: info@irahelp.com

Twitter: @theslottreport

Facebook: AmericasIRAExperts

LinkedIn: Ed Slott and Company

YouTube: EdSlottandCompanyIRA

Notes